Santa Monica Public Library

I SMP 00 1455480 Y

D1006622

MONTANA BRANCH
SANTA MONICA PUBLIC LIBRARY
OCT   2005

JOHN
HANCOCK
SIGNER FOR INDEPENDENCE

SPECIAL LIVES IN HISTORY THAT BECOME

Signature LIVES

JOHN

HANCOCK
SIGNER FOR INDEPENDENCE

by Barbara A. Somervill

Content Adviser: Julie Richter, Ph.D.,
Independent Scholar and Consultant,
Colonial Williamsburg Foundation

Reading Adviser: Rosemary G. Palmer, Ph.D.,
Department of Literacy, College of Education,
Boise State University

COMPASS POINT BOOKS ✦ MINNEAPOLIS, MINNESOTA

Compass Point Books
3109 West 50th Street, #115
Minneapolis, MN 55410

Visit Compass Point Books on the Internet at *www.compasspointbooks.com*
or e-mail your request to *custserv@compasspointbooks.com*

Managing Editor: Catherine Neitge
Lead Designer: Jaime Martens
Photo Researcher: Svetlana Zhurkina
Cartographer: XNR Productions, Inc.
Educational Consultant: Diane Smolinski

Art Director: Keith Griffin
Production Director: Keith McCormick
Creative Director: Terri Foley

Library of Congress Cataloging-in-Publication Data
Somervill, Barbara A.
 John Hancock / by Barbara A. Somervill.
   p. cm—(Signature lives)
 Includes bibliographical references and index.
 ISBN 0-7565-0980-7 (hardcover)
 1. Hancock, John, 1737-1793—Juvenile literature. 2. Statesmen—United
States—Biography—Juvenile literature. 3. United States. Declaration of
Independence—Signers—Biography—Juvenile literature. 4. United
States—History—Revolution, 1775-1783—Juvenile literature. I. Title.
II. Series.
 E302.6.H23S66 2005
 973.3'092—dc22   2004017196

© 2005 by Compass Point Books
All rights reserved. No part of this book may be reproduced without written permission
from the publisher. The publisher takes no responsibility for the use of any of the
materials or methods described in this book, nor for the products thereof.
Printed in the United States of America.

REVOLUTIONARY WAR ERA

The American Revolution created heroes—and traitors—
who shaped the birth of a new nation: the United States
of America. "Taxation without representation" was a serious
problem for the American colonies during the late 1700s.
Great Britain imposed harsh taxes and didn't give the
colonists a voice in their own government. The colonists
rebelled and declared their independence from Britain—
the war was on.

John Hancock

Table of Contents

1 STAND UP FOR FREEDOM

ॐᵉᵍᐟᐣᐣ

*J*uly 2, 1776, was a hot, humid day in colonial Philadelphia, Pennsylvania. The air was thick and moist inside the meeting room of the State House. John Hancock of Massachusetts, president of the Second Continental Congress, called the meeting to order. Men representing each of the 13 North American colonies took their seats.

A hush fell over the men as Thomas Jefferson of Virginia read:

> We hold these truths to be self-evident, that all men are created equal, that they are endowed by their Creator with certain unalienable Rights, that among these are Life, Liberty and the pursuit of Happiness ...

John Hancock (seated) received the Declaration of Independence from Thomas Jefferson and other members of the committee.

9 ॐ

Richard Henry Lee (1732-1794) belonged to a famous Virginia family known for public service. Lee served in the House of Burgesses and openly opposed British taxes. He called the Townshend Acts "arbitrary, unjust, and destructive." Lee signed the Declaration of Independence.

For three days, the delegates discussed, shouted, and expressed their opinions. Change this! Reword that! Adjust that paragraph! The members wanted the document to be perfect. It had to express their views and the views of many colonial citizens about British rule.

In June, Richard Henry Lee of Virginia had introduced a resolution that the American colonies should be free and independent states. The Continental Congress then appointed a committee to write a document expressing the colonists' views toward their rule by Great Britain.

The Continental Congress included names that have filled American history books: Thomas Jefferson, John Adams, and Benjamin Franklin. Other men were there, too. They were doctors, merchants, lawyers, and farmers. They had wives and children, houses and businesses. Their names have been all but forgotten over time: Abraham Clark, George Ross, and William Ellery. These men represented the hopes of their colonies' citizens, who wanted to be free of British rule. They willingly risked everything they had to work toward the goal of independence.

On this hot July day, the first draft of the document

was presented to the members of the Continental Congress. Then, on July 4, 1776, the delegates finally approved this most amazing document—the Declaration of Independence.

John Hancock served as president of the Second Continental Congress.

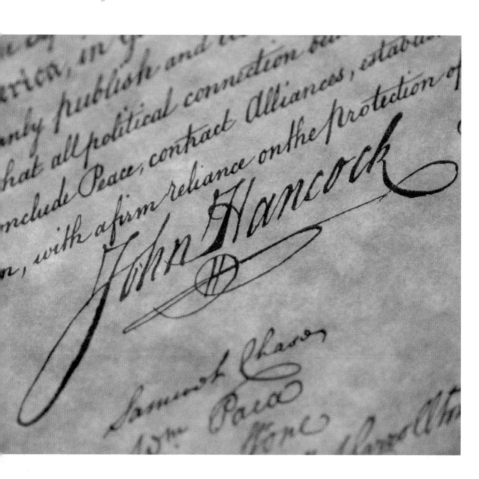

John Hancock signed his name with a flourish.

Then the delegates left, asking John Hancock and the Continental Congress's secretary, Charles Thomson, to make the approved changes. The quiet scratching of quill on parchment became the only sound in the near-empty meeting room. Gone were the shouts and whispers. Leather boots no longer shuffled on the wooden floors. Chairs and benches did not creak beneath the weight of shifting bodies.

John Hancock considered the paper he was

about to sign. He dipped his quill into black India ink. He wrote his signature, large, bold, and clear, directly beneath the last sentence.

It is said that Hancock declared, "There, King George will be able to read that without his spectacles." Hancock was the only member of the Continental Congress to sign the declaration that fourth day of July, now called Independence Day. Thomson added his signature on that first Declaration of Independence only as a witness.

By signing the Declaration of Independence, John Hancock became a traitor in British eyes. This was nothing new for Hancock. He had already been tried for smuggling and found not guilty. He had earlier been accused of acts of high treason against King George III and narrowly escaped arrest.

Signing the declaration was different, though. There was no escaping the fact that here was his name, his signature, on this document that would enrage the British. If the British arrested him, Hancock would be hanged for treason. Instead, Hancock became an American patriot and a founding father of the United States of America. ॐ

2 THE YOUNG JOHN HANCOCK

The Hancock family held a proud place in the history of the Massachusetts Colony. Grandfather, father, and son were all named John, and they served actively in their communities.

In the early 1700s, Hancock's grandfather, the Reverend John Hancock, preached from the pulpit of the North Precinct Congregational Church in the area near Boston that became Lexington. As a minister, Hancock's grandfather provided the moral fiber of his community. He was so well respected that people called him Bishop, although no such rank existed in the church. He married Elizabeth Clark, and their first child, a son, was also given the name John.

Eventually, the second John Hancock followed in his father's footsteps, from Harvard College into another Congregational church. The second Reverend Hancock married Mary Hawke, a farmer's daughter. The couple had three children: Mary, born in 1735; John in 1737; and Ebenezer in 1741. The family lived in Braintree (now Quincy), Massachusetts, which was a small village about eight miles (13 kilometers) from Boston.

Braintree was a typical colonial New England town. The town's center featured a common green where cows and sheep grazed. Around the green stood the church, homes, and businesses. Shops might have included a grocery, a blacksmith, a cobbler for shoes, a tanner for leather, a carpenter, and a miller of grain.

Braintree was a productive farming community, too. Local farmers grew wheat, barley, hay, and corn. In fact, corn provided the basic food for the colonists in this area. Fresh meat rarely appeared on the family dinner table unless it came from hunting. Local woods were filled with deer, ducks, geese, and wild turkeys. Farmers also fished to provide food for their families. Each fall, colonists slaughtered pigs or cattle and preserved the meat by storing it in casks filled with spices, salt, and water. Throughout the winter, families ate this salt pork or corned beef, the only butchered meat that could be kept without refrigeration. Women planted gardens with onions, potatoes, carrots, cabbage, parsnips, and peas.

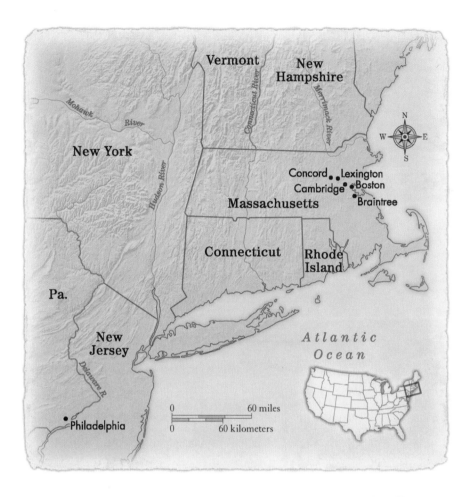

Braintree was a tight-knit community where everyone knew each other. The Reverend John Hancock and his family lived beside the common. Their neighbors included the Adams and Quincys, two well-known Massachusetts families.

John Hancock's early childhood was like that of other boys of the era. He chased after John Adams and the Quincy boys, who were older than Hancock.

John Hancock spent his early years in Braintree, Massachusetts, near Boston. The part of Braintree where he lived split off to form the town of Quincy in 1792.

The lads whooped and hollered through the nearby woods. In the summer, they swam in a stream. Winters brought sledding, skating, and snowball fights.

In those days, only towns with 50 or more families had schools and teachers for their children. Small villages like Braintree relied on schooling in the parlor or kitchen of a local woman. These were called dame schools. At 5 years old, John entered a dame school run by Mrs. Belcher, who taught him reading, writing, and arithmetic.

At first, life was simple for John as he played, did chores, and attended school. That changed quickly, however. When John was 7 years old, his father died unexpectedly. As a minister, John's father was well respected but poorly paid. Mrs. Hancock and the children were left with no money. John's grandfather—the Bishop—decided to take the family into his home. He wanted to train young John to become a minister, as was expected of the boy. However, John's Uncle Thomas, a wealthy Boston merchant, had other ideas.

Thomas heard about the problems his dead brother's family faced. He and his wife, Lydia, had no children. More important, Thomas needed an heir to inherit the House of Hancock, his thriving Boston business. With Mary Hancock's permission, Thomas and Lydia adopted John. They also gave Mary money to support herself and her other

Thomas Hancock was one of the richest men in Boston.

children. Once John left his mother's home, very little is heard again of his family.

Thomas promised to have John follow in his father's footsteps and attend college at Harvard in nearby Cambridge, Massachusetts. However, Thomas did not intend for John to become a preacher.

John's new life in Boston was much different from the quiet village life he had enjoyed. Boston was a bustling port city. More than 500 ships sailed into Boston Harbor each year. The ships carried whale oil, timber, fur pelts, and other raw materials to England. On the return trip, the cargo holds were filled with furniture, china, spices, tea, works of art, and dozens of other items. Near the wharves were warehouses for storing goods and retail dealers for supplying ships with rope, sails, and other fittings.

A replica of Thomas and John Hancock's grand home was built for the World's Columbian Exposition of 1893 in Chicago. It served as a museum during the world's fair.

Boston also boasted churches with tall steeples, taverns and inns, and shops selling all sorts of wares. The city and its merchants prospered. Yet, the British government made sure that it got

its share of Boston's profits. A good deal of Massachusetts's wealth found its way back to England in the form of taxes.

Among the richest of Boston's merchants was Thomas Hancock. He had earned his money through hard work. As a young man, Thomas served as an apprentice to a bookseller. When he was 21, he started his own business as a publisher and bookseller.

Thomas Hancock had his portrait painted by famous colonial artist John Singleton Copley.

From books, Thomas expanded to selling all sorts of necessary goods, from cloth and paper, to fish, rum, and tea. He built the House of Hancock from the ground up. He earned the elegant life he lived.

The Hancock home on Beacon Hill was possibly the finest house in Boston. At night, candles gleamed from the home's many glass windows. The rooms featured mahogany furniture, velvet curtains, and wallpaper, a rare and expensive decorating touch.

Aunt Lydia and Uncle Thomas cared for John as if he were their own child. Lydia dressed John in the fashion of the day. He wore velvet breeches, lace-trimmed shirts, and fine leather shoes with silver

Harvard College was nearly 115 years old when John Hancock started his studies there.

buckles. Young John attended the Boston Latin School, where he improved the basic educational skills of reading, penmanship, arithmetic, and Latin.

Away from school, John learned the business of selling, shipping, and making money. Thomas and John rode in an elegant carriage over Boston's cobblestone streets. They watched goods unloaded on the Hancock wharf. They inspected cargoes of tea, cloth, plates, glass, wine, and rum in warehouses owned by the House of Hancock.

When John was 13 years old, Thomas and Lydia sent him to Harvard College to finish his education. Founded in 1636, Harvard was the oldest college in the colonies. In the 1750s, when John was there, Harvard had about 50 students, young men in their teens. Harvard students studied Latin and Greek. They read classic poetry and the writings of political thinkers and philosophers. They learned about science, debated politics, and developed long-term friendships.

A Harvard graduation ceremony in the 1750s was much like a county fair. Farmers set up stalls to sell apples, honey, corn, and other produce. Acrobats and jugglers entertained the crowds. Music filled the streets, setting toes to tapping and hands a-clapping. Young men took their chances at games of dice and cards.

Some historians believe that Harvard was a hotbed of revolution. Harvard's president encouraged students to think, debate, and challenge the political and social thinking of the time. The school's graduates included many active revolutionaries, including John Adams, Samuel Adams, Thomas Cushing, Elbridge Gerry, and James Otis. These men led the revolutionary movement against the British in Massachusetts.

John graduated in 1754. For John Hancock, graduation was simply the next step in his neatly arranged life. He left the classrooms of Harvard for the House of Hancock.

3 THE HOUSE OF HANCOCK

❦

Working in the House of Hancock's counting room helped John Hancock understand the world of business. He learned about profits and losses, keeping accounts, buying and selling goods, and banking. The company owned ships, a wharf in Boston, shops, and warehouses. The young Hancock learned how to manage his uncle's massive business.

John also learned how to dress for his role, something his Uncle Thomas believed that wealthy merchants should do. Both he and John wore elegant wool coats and shirts of fine, soft linen. Ruffles and lace graced their necks and wrists. Silver buckles and buttons sparkled on their shoes and coats. Ready for business, uncle and nephew traveled each morning to the House of Hancock.

Goods shipped to and from the House of Hancock passed through the Custom House dock on London's River Thames.

They spent their days at work, although they actually worked only in the morning. Each afternoon, John and Thomas headed to the Merchant's Club or a local tavern or coffeehouse. John discovered that having business friends was an important part of running the House of Hancock. Lunch, business, and politics filled most afternoons. Together, merchants dined on wild turkey, salmon, chicken, and venison. They drank ale or wine. They devoured apple tarts, plum cakes, and cherry pies. Uncle and nephew often did not return home until late in the evening.

London in the 1760s stood at the start of the Industrial Revolution. Men, women, and children worked 10 to 12 hours a day in textile mills and factories. They received little pay and suffered dreadful conditions, working seven days a week. While the working class struggled, the rich lived idle, comfortable lives. Many wealthy people never worked a day in their lives.

In 1760, the House of Hancock's success depended on close ties to London's merchants. To better understand how the English conducted business, John went to live in London. There, he met and worked with British business agents. He became friends with the British merchants who both bought from and sold goods to the Hancocks.

After less than two years in England, John returned to Boston. Thomas Hancock had taken ill. When he arrived, John found his weak, sickly uncle looking much

older than his 58 years. John quickly put his knowl-edge to work, running the business day to day. On January 1, 1763, Thomas made John a partner. Thomas wrote to his various business associates:

The Royal Exchange in Cheapside, London, where Hancock spent about two years

> *Gent'n*
> *I am to acquaint you that I have at last Got my affairs into such a Scituation, as that I have this Day Taken my Nephew Mr. John Hancock, into Partnership with me having had long Experience of his Up-rightness & great Abilities for Business, as that I can heartily Recommend him to Your Friendship and Correspondence …*
> > *Your most Obed't Serv't*
> > *Thomas Hancock*

*Boston Harbor
in 1764*

For more than a year, John ran the House of Hancock as managing partner. Thomas's health continued to fail, and he became bedridden in early 1764. Thomas died later that year, and John inherited tremendous wealth. In all, he received the equivalent of many millions of dollars in today's currency and all the company's holdings. In addition, he inherited 22,000 acres (8,800 hectares) of land in Massachusetts and the neighboring colony of Connecticut and what is now Maine.

John Hancock was generous with his wealth. Most Boston houses were built of wood, and fire constantly threatened the city. So Hancock bought a fire engine for Boston. Through the years, he also supported a number of churches besides the one he and Aunt Lydia attended. During cold winters, Hancock provided firewood, clothing, and food for poor families. He set up several young clerks in their own businesses. In every way, John Hancock lived up to his family's tradition of community service.

Most colonial businessmen were supposed to pay taxes on their earnings to the British government. In 1733, the government had passed a tax law called the Molasses Act. This act prohibited the colonists from buying molasses from the Dutch or French West Indies and forced them to buy it from the British West Indies. Merchants who brought molasses into Boston or turned the molasses into rum for shipping abroad paid a sugar tax to Great Britain.

Every colonial kitchen had a crock of molasses in the pantry. Refined white sugar was very expensive, and few colonists could afford it. Instead, molasses—a liquid "brown" sugar— was used in baking, puddings, and baked beans. Molasses was sometimes used to sweeten tea or coffee and in making rum.

According to the Molasses Act, Boston merchants owed "the sum of nine pence, money of Great Britain, … for every gallon [of rum]: and upon all molasses or syrups, the sum of six pence of like money for every gallon."

Molasses was the main ingredient in rum, and rum provided huge profits for Boston's businessmen. Rum made from smuggled molasses—on which no tax was paid—made even more money. John Hancock became a molasses smuggler to ensure a bigger profit. He wasn't alone. Most molasses and rum traders smuggled at least some of their shipments into Boston.

Many goods— legal and illegal —were shipped through the busy French port of Marseille.

The House of Hancock also bought goods from Spain and France, which was against British law. By law, only wine and salt could be bought from countries other than Great Britain. However, sales of Spanish and French wine, cloth, lace, glassware, and other goods kept Hancock shops full of customers.

John Hancock ignored the import laws because he believed he was doing the right thing. Many colonists depended on him for jobs and bought goods from his stores for their families. By providing the best and cheapest products, he kept people employed and families well supplied.

As Great Britain forced higher taxes on the colonies, many colonists spoke out against their rulers. The Hancocks had always been loyal to their king and mother country. However, as British rule grew more demanding, John Hancock's thoughts changed. He became a revolutionary. 🍂

4 TAX TROUBLES

❧⟨✦⟩❧

Serious problems with British taxes began just after the French and Indian War (1754–1763). In this war, the British fought the French over control of North American land. The conflict spread to other countries around the world, where it was known as the Seven Years' War.

The British found that fighting a war far from home was expensive. They had to ship, clothe, feed, arm, and pay soldiers. In 1763, Great Britain decided that the colonies should help with war costs by paying taxes. The British looked at the colonies as a bottomless piggybank. Many colonists, however, believed they should be treated as more of an equal partner within the British Empire since they had helped defeat the French and her allies.

A portrait of the British ruler, King George III, by famous painter Thomas Gainsborough

Although taxing the colonies actually began with the Molasses Act of 1733, the British hadn't collected as much money as they'd hoped. Ships carrying molasses and rum were supposed to be inspected by customs agents, but those agents lived in London, an ocean away from Boston. As a result, smuggling had become a common event in Boston Harbor. The British government realized it was missing out on huge amounts of money.

In 1763, the job of customs agents changed. The British government insisted that agents set up customs houses in colonial ports and inspect all cargoes. Agents charged and collected duties, or taxes, on all sugar products. All of this made smuggling much harder.

Then in 1764, the British replaced the Molasses Act with the Sugar Act. Now Britain charged tax on all imported sugars and wine. Plus, they added taxes on some non-sugar items, such as indigo, coffee, silk, and other imported textiles.

Also in 1764, the British government tightened the clamps on colonies printing their own money. The Currency Act made paying debts in England with colonial paper money illegal. Only British pounds sterling could be used to pay debts.

For the first time in his adult life, John Hancock faced money problems. His customers paid for their purchases with goods or in colonial currency.

However, he had to buy new products and pay shipping or warehousing in British pounds.

The following year, the British passed another tax. The Stamp Act required colonists to buy a stamp for all documents. This included bills, bail bonds, deeds, wills, college diplomas, newspapers, leaflets, books, almanacs, and pamphlets. A tax was also charged on playing cards and dice.

For John Hancock, stamps had to appear on the bills he sent to customers and the bills he owed to suppliers. Without a stamp, no business could run, no printed material be sold, and no property be exchanged. The colonists, Hancock included, burned with anger.

The citizens of Boston rallied against the hated Stamp Act.

The Stamp Act was set to become official on November 1, 1765. Colonists from New England to Georgia resented the idea that Britain could tax them. They complained of taxation without representation. After all, no colonial members sat in the British Parliament. Besides, while the Sugar Act only

An angry mob protests the Stamp Act by throwing stamped documents onto a bonfire in Boston.

affected wealthy businessmen, the Stamp Act reached into the pockets of everyday citizens.

Colonial merchants rebelled. They refused to pay the stamp tax or to buy British goods. Massachusetts asked for help from other colonies. New York and Pennsylvania agreed to join a boycott of British goods.

The boycott was not a simple matter. It stopped the import of furniture, cloth, wine, tea, coffee, and even food needed in the colonies.

John Hancock did not want to take part in the boycott. He wanted to remain loyal to Great Britain. However, he realized that the Stamp Act could put many shopkeepers, craftsmen, and professional people out of business. In the end, he joined the boycott with his fellow Boston merchants. Hancock wrote to his London agent, saying that the Stamp Act "is a cruel hardship upon us." He claimed that paying the tax was equal to becoming a slave to England.

The boycott of British goods succeeded. Many British merchants also complained about the Stamp Act, which was repealed less than six months after it went into effect.

Although the British seemed to cave in on the Stamp Act, they were not done levying taxes. Starting in 1766, the government passed three new tax laws. The first, the Declaratory Act, stated that Parliament still had the right to tax its citizens —and that included colonists in North America. Then Parliament passed a new Sugar Act. This act reduced the tax on molasses by a penny a gallon but added a tax on coffee.

The third tax law, passed in 1767, was the Townshend Revenue Act. This law placed duties on tea, glass, paper, red and white lead for paints, and painters' colors. A tax on tea was a terrible inconvenience. Tea was the most popular drink in the colonies.

The new taxes affected all Boston citizens. The added taxes increased the sale price of tea, coffee, paper, paints, and cloth. Poor citizens had to go without these items. Fewer people could buy imported goods, so sales at the House of Hancock dropped. Lower sales affected profits. In addition, reduced sales meant that Hancock needed fewer salesclerks in his stores.

To overcome the effect of British taxes, John Hancock, like many other shipping barons, smuggled non-British goods into Boston. Determined to collect their tax money, though, the British started

James Otis (1725-1783), although a rebel, was torn between being a patriotic colonist and a loyal British subject. A political leader and lawyer in colonial Massachusetts, Otis favored colonial representatives in the British Parliament over freedom from Great Britain. He also represented colonial smugglers and tax evaders in court. Otis died in 1783 when struck by lightning.

inspecting cargoes before dockworkers began to unload the goods.

Taxes and British rule dominated conversations in taverns and coffee-houses. Hancock decided to take action. He became involved in Boston politics. He ran for and was elected to the Boston Town Council. He joined known rebels Samuel Adams, James Otis, and Thomas Cushing on the council. These men changed Hancock from a loyal British subject to a colonial patriot.

John Hancock was denied a seat on the Governor's Council.

The Massachusetts General Court chose John Hancock for the Governor's Council. However, Francis Bernard, the royal governor, did not like Hancock. He knew Hancock smuggled to avoid taxes, and resented the young man's wealth and popularity. Governor Bernard refused to allow Hancock on the Governor's Council. Hancock shrugged off the insult. He had plenty to do between Boston politics and the House of Hancock.

Increased British customs inspections eventually created serious problems for Hancock. In April 1768,

Hancock's ship, *Lydia*, anchored in Boston Harbor. The next day, two customs agents arrived to check the cargo. Hancock refused to allow them aboard because they did not have their official papers. Late that night, another agent tried to sneak aboard the *Lydia*. He, too, lacked the needed papers, so Hancock had him removed from the ship.

By the time the correct papers were presented, Hancock's crew had already unloaded the cargo. No inspection meant no tax collected. However, agents now put Hancock's ships under a close watch.

British agents checked cargo not only at the London Customs House on the River Thames, but also in the colonies.

A few weeks later the *Liberty*, another of Hancock's ships, arrived carrying a valuable load of Spanish wine. The ship docked at night, and when customs agents arrived the next morning, the ship was more than half empty. A few weeks later, a customs agent said he was forcibly held on the ship that night and heard cargo being unloaded. He said he had been threatened not to tell anyone. The British seized the ship and accused John Hancock of smuggling and dodging taxes.

Boston seethed with anger over the British taking the *Liberty*. Roving mobs attacked British officers and agents with sticks and clubs. A mob burned a boat owned by a customs agent. Still, the British held fast to the *Liberty*.

The British court fined Hancock an enormous amount of money, about $1 million in today's currency. The court filed official charges against Hancock. To avoid jail, he paid a huge bail—more than 30 times the yearly salary of most workers. John Adams, an old friend and future U.S. president, served as Hancock's lawyer. Adams put forth the defense of taxation without representation.

The Hancock trial roused public opinion against the British. The House of Hancock employed many people and sold goods to nearly everyone in Boston. Hancock himself was a popular Boston figure. As the trial dragged on, angry mobs roamed Boston

British soldiers arrived to patrol the streets of Boston, much to the dismay of the colonial citizens.

streets causing trouble. They let the British know that they supported John Hancock.

The British felt the need to boost their defenses in Boston. The Royal Navy brought in five ships.

Soldiers arrived to patrol Boston streets. The city looked like an armed camp. On the one side were Boston's angry citizens. On the other stood uniformed soldiers bearing muskets.

In January 1769, Massachusetts merchants again called for a boycott of British goods. Every colony except New Hampshire followed suit, and by the end of the year British merchants had lost a nearly catastrophic amount of sales.

Early that same year, the British dropped all charges against John Hancock. He was again selected to serve on the Governor's Council, and once again, he was rejected. In August, Governor Bernard returned to London. He happily left Boston, its rebels, and the maddening John Hancock behind him.

What happened to the missing wine from the *Liberty?* That was securely stored in Hancock's wine cellar. ✑

5 A Massacre and a Tea Party

Chapter

❧❧❧

By 1770, British soldiers dressed in bright red coats guarded the main streets. Angry mobs roamed Boston's back alleys. British sailors filled the dockside taverns, while Boston citizens drank their ale in town. Citizens claimed that soldiers fired their muskets at them. Some said they had been poked with bayonets. Bostonians grew fearful and angry. The situation was a powder keg waiting to explode.

The explosion came on March 5, 1770. On that night, an apprentice and his friend teased a British soldier on guard duty. They taunted the guard, calling him lobsterback (because of his red coat) and daring him to shoot them. Fed up with the flurry of insults, the guard knocked the apprentice down with the butt of his rifle. A mob quickly gathered,

A 1770 engraving by Paul Revere sensationalizes the skirmish that became known as the Boston Massacre.

hurling insults and snowballs at the soldier.

The British guard called for support. It came from Captain Thomas Preston and seven soldiers of England's 29th company. The rowdy mob shoved and jostled the soldiers. The mob threw snowballs and sticks, and one guard opened fire. Several more shots rang out. Five Bostonians were killed: Crispus Attucks, a free African-American; James Caldwell, a sailor; Patrick Carr, an Irish immigrant; Samuel Gray, a rope weaver; and 17-year-old Samuel Maverick. Several other men were wounded.

News of the killings, which became known as the Boston Massacre, spread from house to house. Church bells pealed throughout Boston. The streets filled with a frenzied mob.

Preston and his men were arrested. The British captain later described the event, in which the British soldiers were not truly at fault. Preston explained that, though armed, his men did not intend to fire on the crowd. The unruly mob forced the British soldiers to open fire. This was not the news Bostonians wanted to hear, even though it was the truth.

Hancock, Samuel Adams, and other Boston leaders were outraged. They ignored the fact that the colonists had started the attack. They were only concerned that the British had killed and wounded Boston citizens. A citizens' committee

Samuel Adams demanded that British troops leave Boston.

demanded that the British withdraw troops from the city.

Boston's leaders delivered this message to the lieutenant governor:

> "That is it the unanimous opinion of this meeting that the inhabitants and soldiery can no longer live together in safety; that nothing can rationally be expected to restore the peace of the town and prevent further blood and carnage, but the immediate removal of the troops; and that we therefore ... pray his Honour, that his power and influence may be exerted for their instant removal."

The soldiers of England's 29th company no longer patrolled Boston's streets—although other British soldiers did. Today, some historians consider the Boston Massacre to be the true start of the American Revolution.

Over the next few years, the British constantly tried to bring Boston's rebels under control. British troops in the streets, the seizing of ships, and higher taxes had no effect. Fiery Samuel Adams and the more peaceful John Hancock rallied the Sons of Liberty, the anti-British political group, to resist. The British knew about the Sons of Liberty but could not act against them. As yet, its members had broken no laws.

One topic that continued to irritate Boston citizens was the tea tax. For several years, Boston colonists resisted Britain's tea tax by refusing to buy tea. The East India Company, the major supplier of tea, lost money. The company's warehouses bulged with bales of unsold tea. Since many British politicians owned shares in the East India Company, such a loss

The Sons of Liberty met in public beneath the Liberty Tree. According to rumor, the British cut down the tree in 1775 because it was a sign of colonial rebellion. Here is an excerpt from Thomas Paine's "Liberty Tree":
... King, Commons and Lords are uniting amain
To cut down this guardian of ours
From the East to the West blow the trumpet to arms
Through the land let the sound of it flee
Let the far and the near all unite with a cheer
In defense of our Liberty Tree ...

THE
ASSOCIATION
OF
THE SONS OF LIBERTY,
OF
NEW-YORK.

IT is effential to the Freedom and Security of a Free People, that no Taxes be impofed upon them but by their own Confent, or their Reprefentatives. For " what Property have they, in that, which another may, by Right, take when he pleafes, to himfelf ?" The Former is the undoubted Birth-right of *Englifhmen*, to fecure which, they expended Millions, and facrificed the Lives of Thoufands. And yet, to the Aftonifhment of all the World, and the Grief of *America*, the Commons of *Great-Britain*, after the Repeal of the memorable and deteftable *Stamp Act*, reaffumed the Power of impofing Taxes on the *American* Colonies, and infifting on it, as a neceffary Badge of Parliamentary Supremacy, paffed a Bill, in the feventh Year of his prefent Majefty's Reign, impofing Duties on all Glafs, Painters Colours, Paper, and Teas, that fhould after the 20th of *November*, 1767, be " imported from *Great-Britain*, into any Co-lony or Plantation in *America*." This Bill, after the Concurrence of the Lords, obtained the Royal Affent. And thus, they, who from Time immemorial, have exercifed the Right of giving to, or withholding from the Crown, their Aids and Subfidies, according to their *own free Will and Pleafure*, fignified by their Repre-fentatives in Parliament, do, by the Act in Queftion, deny us, their Brethren in *America*, the Enjoyment of the fame Right. As this Denial, and the Execution of that Act, involves our Slavery, and would fap the Foundation of our Freedom, whereby we fhould become Slaves to our Brethren and Fellow Subjects, born to no greater Stock of Freedom than the *Americans*; the Merchants and Inhabitants of this City, in Conjunc-tion with the Merchants and Inhabitants of the ancient *American* Colonies, entered into an Agreement to decline a Part of their Commerce with *Great-Britain*, until the abovementioned Act fhould be totally re-pealed. This Agreement operated fo powerfully to the Difadvantage of the Manufacturers of *England*, that many of them were unemployed. To appeafe their Clamours, and to provide the Subfiftence for them, which the Non-Importation Agreement had deprived them of, the Parliament in 1770, repealed fo much of the Revenue Act as impofed a Duty on Glafs, Painters Colours, and Paper, and left the Duty on Tea, as *a Teft of the Parliamentary Right to Tax us*. The Merchants of the Cities of *New-York* and *Philadelphia*, hav-ing ftrictly adhered to the Agreement, fo far as it related to the Importation of Articles fubject to an *Ame-rican* Duty; have convinced the Miniftry, that fome other Meafure muft be adopted, to execute Parliamentary Supremacy, over this Country; and to remove the Diftrefs brought on the *Eaft India* Company, by the ill Policy of that Act. Accordingly, to increafe the Temptation, to the Shippers of Tea from *England*, an Act of Parliament paffed the laft Seffion, which gives the whole Duty on Tea, the Company were fubject to pay, upon the Importation of it into *England*, to the Purchafers, and Exporters; and when the Company have Ten Millions of Pounds of Tea, in their Warehoufes, exclufive of the Quantity they may want to fhip, they are allowed to export Tea, difcharged from the Payment of that Duty, with which they were before charge-able. In Hopes of Aid in the Execution of this Project, by the Influence of the Owners of the *American* Ships, Application was made, by the Company, to the Captains of thofe Ships, to take the Tea on Freight ; but they virtuoufly rejected it. Still determined on the Scheme, they have chartered Ships to bring over the Tea to this Country, which may be hourly expected, to make an important Trial of our Virtue. If they fucceed in the Sale of that Tea, we fhall have no Property that we can call our own, and then we may bid adieu to *American* Liberty.——Therefore, to prevent a Calamity, which, of all others, is the moft to be dreaded,——Slavery, and its terrible Concomitants,—We the Subfcribers, being influenced from a Regard to Liberty, and difpofed to ufe all lawful Endeavours, in our Power, to defeat the pernicious Project, and to tranf-mit to our Pofterity, thofe Bleffings of Freedom, which our Anceftors have handed down to us; and to contri-bute to the Support of the Common Liberties of *America*, which are in danger to be fubverted, DO, for thofe important Purpofes, agree to affociate together, under the Name and Stile of the SONS of LIBERTY, of NEW-YORK, and engage our Honour, to and with each other, faithfully to obferve and perform the following RESOLUTIONS, Viz.

1ft. RESOLVED, That whoever fhall aid, or abet, or in any Manner affift, in the Introduction of Tea, from any Place whatfoever, into this Colony, while it is fubject by a *Britifh* Act of Parliament, to the Payment of a Duty, for the Purpofe of raifing a Revenue in *America*, he fhall be deemed, an Enemy to the Liberties of *America*.

2d. RESOLVED, That whoever fhall be aiding, or affifting, in the Landing, or carting of fuch Tea, from any Ship, or Veffel, or fhall hire any Houfe, Storehoufe, or Cellar, or any Place whatfoever, to depofit the Tea, fubject to a Duty as aforefaid, he fhall be deemed, an Enemy to the Liberties of *America*.

3d. RESOLVED, That whoever fhall fell, or buy, or in any Manner contribute to the Sale, or Purchafe of Tea, fubject to a Duty as aforefaid, or fhall aid, or abet, in tranfporting fuch Tea, by Land, or Water, from this City, until the 7th. Geo. III. Chap. 46, commonly called the Revenue Act, fhall be totally, and clearly repealed, he fhall be deemed, an Enemy to the Liberties of *America*.

4th. RESOLVED, That whether the Duties on Tea, impofed by this Act, be paid in *Great Britain*, or in *America*, our Liberties are equally affected.

5th. RESOLVED, That whoever fhall tranfgrefs any of thefe Refolutions, we will not deal with, or employ, or have any Connection with him.

NEW-YORK, November 29, 1773.

A proclamation by the Sons of Liberty condemned the British tax on tea and those colonists who supported it. The resolutions demanded a colonial boycott of imported British tea.

of money was not welcome.

The British government passed the Tea Act of 1773. The law allowed the East India Company to sell its tea without paying a large tax to England.

The law also let the company sell tea directly to the colonists. This law gave the East India Company an unfair advantage over colonial merchants. It could sell its tea at a price even cheaper than the colonies could smuggle it.

The daring raid known as the Boston Tea Party took less than three hours.

Shopkeepers, even ones as wealthy as John Hancock, would lose business. Many shops would close. Hancock ordered his ships to refuse cargoes

of East India Company tea, but other ships brought the tea. As those ships lay in Boston Harbor, the patriots planned a little tea party.

On December 16, 1773, a group of rebels dressed themselves like Mohawk Indians. The men slipped aboard the cargo ships and dumped 342 chests of tea into Boston Harbor. That tea was worth the equivalent of $1 million in today's currency.

British officials claimed that Hancock stood guard while the rebels held their tea party. That seems unlikely. Hancock was too recognizable, and he was beginning to suffer from attacks of gout. Spending an evening on a wharf during a cold Boston night would have been foolish. However, Hancock did know about and approve of the Boston Tea Party.

In a letter to his London agent dated December 21, 1773, Hancock said,

> *"Every effort was made to Induce the consignees to return it [the tea] from whence it came ... [and] in a very few Hours the whole of the Tea on Board ... was thrown into the salt water."*

After that, Hancock shipped the British tea in his own warehouses back to England. He settled his accounts with British merchants and put his ships up for sale. He had decided to stop trading with the British. ꧁

6 WAR BEGINS

Chapter

❧❧❧

The British government reacted to the Boston Tea Party with anger. To punish Bostonians, the British passed the Coercive Acts, a number of laws that the colonists called the Intolerable Acts. The British government closed Boston Harbor to shipping, which hurt the citizens. Food shortages sent prices soaring, and many went hungry.

Another of the Coercive Acts annulled the Massachusetts charter and colonial self-government. It gave the king sole power to appoint representatives to the colonial council instead of holding elections. People who wanted a greater say in government found themselves with even less of a voice. More than ever, Boston's taxpayers suffered from taxation without representation.

A portrait of General Thomas Gage, the British military governor of Massachusetts, by John Singleton Copley

Another law allowed British colonial officials to be tried in England rather than the colonies. This allowed the officials to do whatever they wished in North America, without fear of judicial reprisal.

Finally, the Quartering Acts forced people to house and feed British soldiers in their own homes. Up until then, the soldiers had not been allowed to stay in private homes. In wealthy towns, soldiers lived and ate in taverns or inns. The townspeople had to pay for the soldiers' housing and food. In other communities, the soldiers lived in private homes. They shared meals with the family. No one wanted an enemy soldier seated at dinner. The Quartering Act proved to be extremely unpopular.

Boston remained under close guard. The British army built a tent city on Boston Common, right in front of John Hancock's Beacon Hill home. The soldiers put up outhouses on the common—a smelly and disgusting situation. The men were loud, filthy, and unruly. The existence of the

> *Parliament passed the Intolerable Acts to punish or control the unruly colonists. The Quartering Act of 1765 was extended and forced colonists to house and feed British soldiers at their own expense. The Boston Port Bill (1774) closed Boston Harbor to all trade after the Boston Tea Party. The Justice Act (1774) allowed British officials to be tried back home in England rather than in the American colonies. The Massachusetts Government Act (1774) put the colony's government in the hands of the appointed British governor.*

camp added pressure to a political volcano set to erupt at any time.

Meanwhile, Hancock's life could not have been busier. His Aunt Lydia had decided it was time for her 36-year-old nephew to marry. She suggested Dorothy Quincy, the daughter of a wealthy family. Dorothy, who was called Dolly, was the youngest of 10 children born to Judge Edmund Quincy and his wife, Elizabeth. Members of the Quincy family, like the Hancocks

Dorothy Quincy was seven years younger than John Hancock.

and Adams, were well known, wealthy, and influential. They were also enthusiastic patriots. Many Boston rebels—John Adams, Samuel Adams, Thomas Cushing, and James Otis, among others— shared tea and cakes in the Quincy's front parlor. Hancock began to court Dolly, but their marriage would not come for another four years.

John Hancock served as a member of the Massachusetts Provincial Congress. The congress, which assumed all powers to rule the colony, believed that war against Great Britain would come and

A 1775 document signed by John Hancock asks commanding officers to report to the Provincial Congress on numbers of men and weapons.

In *Provincial Congress,*

Cambridge, *February* 14, 1775.

*W*HEREAS it appears necessary for the Defence of the Lives, Liberties, and Properties of the Inhabitants of this Province, that this Congress on the firſt Day of their next Seſſion, ſhould be made fully acquainted with the Number and Military Equipments of the Militia, and Minute Men in this Province; and alſo the Town Stock of Ammunition in each Town and Diſtrict :—

It is therefore *RESOLVED*, That it be and it is hereby recommended, to the commanding Officers of each Regiment of Minute Men, that now is or ſhall be formed in this Province, that they review the ſeveral Companies in their reſpective Regiments, or cauſe them to be reviewed, and take an exact State of their Numbers, and Equipment, —and where there is any Company that is not incorporated into a Regiment, the commanding Officer thereof ſhall review the ſeveral Companies, or cauſe them to be reviewed, and take a like State of their Numbers and Equipment.—And it is alſo recommended to the Colonels or commanding Officers of each Regiment of Militia in this Province, that they review the ſeveral Companies in their reſpective Regiments, or cauſe them to be reviewed, and take a State of their Numbers and Accoutrements ; which ſaid State of the Minute Men and Militia, ſhall be by ſaid Officers returned in Writing to this Congreſs, on the firſt Day of their Seſſion after the Adjournment.——

And it is further *RESOLVED*, That it be recommended to the Select-Men of each Town and Diſtrict in the Province, that on the ſame Day they make return in Writing of the State of the Town and Diſtrict Stock of Ammunition, and War-like Stores to this Congreſs.

Signed by Order of the Provincial Congreſs,

JOHN HANCOCK, Preſident.

A true Extract from the Minutes,

BENJAMIN LINCOLN, Secretary.

began planning. Hancock became head of the Committee of Safety, which prepared the colony for war. The committee collected bandages, ammunition, rifles, and medicine for the upcoming battle.

He even arranged for his men to steal four

cannons from the British army in Boston. This was a dangerous, but surprisingly effective, action. Slowly, the rebels built up military supplies in a storehouse in Concord, Massachusetts.

The more active Hancock became against the British, the more General Thomas Gage, Britain's military governor of Massachusetts, despised him as a traitor to the king. British troops on patrol sang a Hancock-related version of "Yankee Doodle Dandy," a popular song of the time:

> *Yankee Doodle came to town*
> *For to buy a firelock;*
> *We will tar and feather him,*
> *And so we will John Hancock.*

With so much unrest in Boston, Hancock sent Lydia and Dolly to nearby Lexington. Hancock warned Dolly's father to leave Boston, too. In April 1775, General Gage finally received official papers for the arrest of John Hancock and Samuel Adams for high treason. The two men fled Boston to join the others, only a few steps ahead of the British soldiers.

Gage sent about 700 soldiers to Concord. The troops had two goals. The first was to arrest Hancock and Adams, and the second was to collect the weapons the patriots had stored in Concord. Rumors spread throughout Boston. The British were on the march.

Paul Revere warned colonists that the British were coming.

Late at night on April 18, Paul Revere, William Dawes, and other messengers rode toward Lexington and Concord. They warned the local people that the British were coming! Church bells pealed. Gunshots echoed the cry. Drums beat the news. Men of all ages, jobs, and abilities headed for Lexington Green.

In Lexington, John Hancock wanted to take a stand and fight the British. Samuel Adams, usually quick to take action, told Hancock not to be fool-ish. While wars needed fighters, they also needed leaders, businessmen, and planners. Adams assured Hancock that he could better serve the patriots' cause alive than dead.

As dawn approached, the Massachusetts min-utemen gathered on Lexington Green. Across the street, Hancock and Adams hopped in a carriage and sped away from the threat of arrest by the British army.

Sylvanus Wood was just 23 years old on April 19, 1775. Later in life, he gave his eyewitness version of the battle:

> *I heard the Lexington bell ring, and fearing there was difficulty there, I immediately arose, took my gun and ... went in haste to Lexington. ...*
>
> *I inquired of Captain Parker, the commander of the Lexington company, what was the news. ... A messenger came up and told the captain that the British troops were within half a mile. Parker immediately turned to his drummer, William Diman, and ordered him to beat to arms. ...*
>
> *Parker says to his men, 'Every man of you who is equipped, follow me; and those of you who are not equipped, go into the meeting-house and furnish yourselves from the magazine, and immediately join the company. ..."*

The British troops approached us rapidly in platoons, with a general officer on horseback at their head. The officer came up to within about two rods of the center of the company. … The officer then swung his sword, and said, 'Lay down your arms, you damned rebels, or you are all dead men. Fire!' Some guns were fired by the British …, but no person was killed or hurt.

Minutemen and British soldiers met to fight on Lexington Green on April 19, 1775.

The next few minutes saw Minutemen jumping over walls and hiding from the trained British soldiers. Shots rang out.

In truth, no two people remembered the events of Lexington the same way. British Army Major John Pitcairn later reported his views of the battle:

Major John Pitcairn of the British Army

A man of the rebels advanced from those that were assembled, had presented his musket and attempted to shoot them, but the piece flashed in the pan. On this I gave directions to the troops to move forward, abut on no account to fire. ... When I came within about 100 yards of them, they began to file off towards some stone walls on our right flank. The Light Infantry, observing this, ran after them. I instantly called to the soldiers not to fire, but surround and disarm them. ... Some of the rebels who had jumped over the wall fired four or five shots at the soldiers, which wounded a man of the Tenth and my horse was wounded in two places ...

On the British side, one man and Major Pitcairn's horse suffered wounds. On the patriots' side, eight Minutemen lay dead and 10 wounded.

Dolly and Lydia saw the entire battle—short as it was—from a house facing Lexington Green. Dolly wrote, "Two men are being brought into the house. One, whose head had been grazed by a ball [bullet], insisted that he was dead, but the other, who was shot through the arm, behaved better." The two women helped bandage and care for the wounded.

The British headed on to Concord to empty the patriot arsenal. By that time, the patriots had chosen hiding places with a clear view of the road. As the British in their red coats left Concord and marched back to Boston, patriot snipers took potshots at their enemy. The unsuspecting British proved an easy target.

Lexington was a defeat for the patriots. Concord was a triumph. The militia had already removed almost everything stored at Concord. Snipers killed 73 British soldiers and wounded another

The military uniforms of the British included a bright red jacket, which led to many nicknames, including redcoats and lobsterbacks. The red color came from madder, which is a vegetable dye. During the time of the Revolution, the brighter the color of fabric dyes and the further from nature the hue, the more expensive they were to produce. So, while browns and blacks were cheap, reds and purples would have been quite costly. Hence their association with royalty. The bright red coats bore a mark of status rather than being a camouflage tactic.

Patriot soldiers chased British troops across North Bridge in Concord.

174. Two dozen British men went missing.

Angry over their defeat, the British poured through towns and villages. They burned homes, stole family treasures, and killed anyone who tried to stop them. The British returned to Boston and the protection of ships' cannons in Boston Harbor.

Hancock and Adams, meanwhile, made a successful escape. Both men had been chosen to represent Massachusetts at the upcoming Second Continental Congress. Hancock and Adams headed to Philadelphia and a prime spot in American history books. ❧

7 Hancock in Charge

❧❧❧

The First Continental Congress had taken place in Philadelphia in 1774. The purpose was to alert King George III to the many complaints the colonists had about British government and its taxes. The king ignored the pleas of his colonial subjects. Now, in 1775, it was too late for pleas to work. King George saw his North American subjects as a bunch of rowdy, disloyal hooligans, rebels, and traitors. The colonists didn't like the king, either.

Virginia's Peyton Randolph had served as president of the First Continental Congress. However, Randolph suffered ill health and could not serve in that position for the Second Continental Congress in May 1775. John Adams, George Washington, and Benjamin Harrison of Virginia suggested John Hancock

A painting of John Hancock by John Singleton Copley, America's first great portrait artist

for president. Hancock was an excellent choice. He was wealthy, so he appealed to other wealthy congressmen. He owned businesses, which gave him something in common with other businessmen in the congress. Hancock received the approval of all representatives.

Hancock was fair, smart, and thoughtful. He considered all viewpoints in every discussion. This was important because the congress was made up of separate colonies and not as united states. Each colony had its own interests, problems, and concerns. Congressmen took sides over every issue: North versus South, business versus agriculture, independent versus loyalist. Yet, as a group, Congress faced serious problems. Hancock's even handling of congressional meetings helped soothe bruised feelings.

It was hard to make headway against the great number of problems that faced the Continental Congress. The first order of business was effectively planning and executing a war. The colonial militia was more a group of men with rifles than an army. The Continental Congress had to build a standing army and appoint a general to lead it. They chose George Washington, much to Hancock's dismay. Hancock saw himself as a general, despite the fact that he had no military experience whatsoever. A fashionable dresser, Hancock may have fancied himself in a general's uniform, but he had no grasp of a military leader's necessary skills.

The army needed lots of things, including a set of rules. A congressional committee developed a list of military guidelines about pay, jobs, and length of service.

Back in Boston, British General Gage held the city in the grip of martial law. He offered a pardon to all the rebels—all except John Hancock and Samuel Adams. Gage said of those two that their "offences are of too [villainous] a nature to admit of an other consideration that of condign [worthy] punishment." Hancock and Adams, Gage decided, did not deserve a pardon. They deserved to be hanged.

A Continental soldier loaded a musket, something that was often in short supply.

Hancock really wanted to join Washington's army, but he had a more important job in Congress. War was big business, and Hancock was a superb businessman. He needed to arrange supplies and pay for the soldiers. Congress decided to raise six companies of riflemen, and Hancock scribbled letter after letter ordering the companies to wherever support might be needed.

From the start of the war,

Benedict Arnold (1741-1801) never could have imagined that his name would become a synonym for traitor. As a patriot, Arnold engaged in a number of battles in New York and New England with mixed success and disappointment. In 1779, the British offered a sullen Arnold a large sum of money and an officer's position. Arnold accepted and became known throughout the new nation as a traitor.

the Continental Army had nothing—no food, clothing, beds, blankets, medicines, weapons, or ammunition. Hancock arranged for the purchase and shipment of these goods throughout the colonies. He developed a supply system for delivering the goods to the troops.

That brought up another problem. The other colonies that had joined in the fight had no money. Hancock, Virginia Representative Carter Braxton, and other wealthy Americans loaned Congress cash from their own pockets to support the Continental Army.

Hancock and Braxton's money could not support a full-scale war, however. So Hancock authorized a committee to raise money from and develop ties with the European countries of France and Spain.

While the politicians busied themselves in Philadelphia, the war slowly progressed. In May 1775, Ethan Allen and Benedict Arnold led an attack at the British Fort Ticonderoga, New York. The colonists captured weapons and cannons. Early the next year, Allen ordered the cannons hauled to Boston to help drive out the British there.

In June, the first true battle between British and patriot troops took place at Breed's Hill, near Boston. In what is known as the Battle of Bunker Hill, the patriots held Breed's Hill against an attack of more than 2,000 British soldiers. The British stormed the hill and were repelled twice. On their third attempt, the British succeeded. By that time, the American troops had run out of ammunition. They could not thwart the oncoming British with

Famous painter John Trumbull served in the Continental Army and witnessed the Battle of Bunker Hill. A detail from his 1786 painting shows the death of American General Warren at the climax of the battle.

stones and clubs. But the British victory proved costly. More than 200 British soldiers were killed and more than 800 wounded. The patriots lost 140 men, and 301 were wounded.

Within three weeks, General George Washington arrived in Massachusetts. The Continental Army had grown to nearly 17,000 troops. However, most were untrained and many unarmed. The colonial effort continued as a disorganized, ragtag group, although they now had a general at their head.

As the war continued, Philadelphia life was hectic and lonely for John Hancock. He realized that he missed Dolly. He proposed marriage and she accepted. On August 28, 1775, Hancock married Dorothy Quincy in Fairfield, Connecticut. The marriage was a grand affair. Reports "devoted pages to describing the glory of the scene and the gorgeousness of the costumes worn upon the occasion; the merrymaking was kept up all night, and

Dorothy Quincy Hancock

in the morning the entire bridal party started for Philadelphia."

As summer gave way to fall, Congress approved a colonial navy of two ships: the *Katy* and the *Washington*. Under the command of Abraham Whipple, the new navy attacked the British ships along the New England coast. In the first naval battle of the war, the *Katy* fired on the British ship *Diana*. Within an hour, the *Diana* broke apart on a rocky island off Rhode Island.

Again, Hancock's experience with the House of Hancock helped the colonial cause. The Hancocks had owned and operated four ships. John Hancock knew the ins and outs of buying and supplying a ship at sea. During the Revolutionary War, Hancock purchased and outfitted 13 more ships for the new Continental Navy.

In Boston, the British bunkered down and strengthened their position. Boston citizens wanted the British gone. At one point, it was suggested that Boston be destroyed to get rid of the hated British. Hancock owned many buildings in the city, but he also wanted the British army out of Boston. He wrote to Thomas Cushing, "Nearly all the property I have in the world is in houses and other real estate in the town of Boston, but if the expulsion of the British army from it … require their being burnt to ashes, issue the order for that purpose immediately."

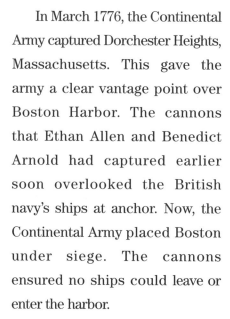

Ethan Allen (1738–1789) led Vermont's Green Mountain Boys, a guerrilla troop active during the Revolution. Allen's daring actions led to the capture of Fort Ticonderoga. Allen, who had little military experience, was a loud-mouthed show-off whose main interest was freedom for Vermont. George Washington said of Allen, "There is an original something about him that commands attention."

In March 1776, the Continental Army captured Dorchester Heights, Massachusetts. This gave the army a clear vantage point over Boston Harbor. The cannons that Ethan Allen and Benedict Arnold had captured earlier soon overlooked the British navy's ships at anchor. Now, the Continental Army placed Boston under siege. The cannons ensured no ships could leave or enter the harbor.

British officers occupied Hancock's home while in Boston. Luckily for John and Dolly, one of John's ship captains had stored much of the furniture elsewhere when Hancock had made his hasty flight to Lexington. The British helped themselves to Hancock's kegs of cider, muskets, glassware, and china. They took bolts of cloth, charcoal, and tore down all the Beacon Hill fences for firewood. Damages and losses to the Beacon Hill mansion and other Hancock properties were considerable.

Threatened by the cannons on Dorchester Hill, the British finally evacuated Boston and set sail for Halifax, Nova Scotia, in Canada. Washington guessed

This engraving of John Hancock's home appeared in Massachusetts Magazine *in 1789.*

that the British would attack New York City next. He was correct. In July 1776, the British war fleet started to arrive in New York Harbor. Thirty ships carried 1,200 cannons that were pointed at New York City, the second largest city in the colonies, after Philadelphia. The ships carried 30,000 soldiers and 10,000 sailors. About 300 ships brought goods to keep the British army well supplied. The patriots faced certain defeat. ❧

Chapter
8 A NEW UNITED STATES

❦

The year 1776 continued to bring bad news. The British had a better-supplied and better-trained army than the colonists. They controlled the seas. To many, the future of the colonies looked bleak.

In the spring, the Continental Congress met to consider the colonies' future. A committee of five men—Thomas Jefferson, Benjamin Franklin, Roger Sherman, John Adams, and Robert Livingston— formed to write a declaration of independence.

The committee produced a rough draft of the declaration. Thomas Jefferson did most of the writing. "Mr. Jefferson," wrote John Adams in his autobiography, "had the reputation of a masterly pen." After several days of arguing over minor points, the congress approved a final version. John Hancock

Three committee members—Franklin (left), Adams, and Jefferson—are shown working on the declaration in this 1900 painting by Jean Leon Gerome Ferris.

> The printed version of the Declaration of Independence bore only two names: John Hancock and Charles Thomson, a witness. Today, about two dozen copies of the original printed version remain in existence.

signed it, and the document quickly headed to the printer.

John Dunlap set the document in type and produced copies to be sent to major cities in all the colonies, for their legislatures to discuss. It took five months for all 56 representatives to sign the formal copy of the declaration. When John Hancock received the copies bearing all the signatures, he forwarded them to each colony. The legislatures had to approve the declaration. Hancock added a letter with each copy. It said, in part:

> *As there is not a more distinguished event in the history of America than the Declaration of her Independence ... it is highly proper that the memory of that transaction, together with the causes that gave rise to it, should be preserved in the most careful manner that can be devised.*

The Declaration of Independence announced to the world that the colonies were now independent states. As president of the Congress, John Hancock became president of those states.

Meanwhile, war news grew bleak. The British took New York City easily, sending General Washington in retreat. November 1776 brought new victories for the British, and more sad defeats for Washington's army. The British triumphed at Fort Washington, New York, and captured 2,800 prisoners as well as cannons, muskets, and ammunition from the Continental Army. The British also won at Fort Lee, New Jersey, and forced Washington's retreat westward toward Trenton, New Jersey.

One of the few remaining copies of the original printed Declaration of Independence

By now, the Continental Army was in a sad state. Many men had died or been wounded in battle. Others had taken sick and could not fight. Some men reached the end of their agreed service and simply headed home. Food grew scarce. As winter approached, the men faced the cold with few blankets and little hope for victory.

In Philadelphia, Congress worried that its temporary capital would soon fall to the British. The British army camped only 20 miles (32 kilometers) from the heart of the city. The Hancocks were concerned. They had enjoyed the birth of a daughter, Lydia Henchman Hancock, in November. Now, with an infant and a wife recovering from childbirth, Hancock planned a withdrawal to Baltimore. The Hancocks and the entire Continental Congress left Philadelphia for Maryland.

> *Early in 1776, Great Britain purchased the military services of nearly 30,000 German soldiers. The soldiers were called Hessians after the parts of Germany they came from. King George III was from Hanover, Germany, so the extra troops were not entirely mercenary. The money King George paid for the troops went directly to German royalty rather than to the soldiers. Most of the men fighting were in debt or drafted, and they saw little, if any, pay for their work.*

The American cause needed a dose of good news. It finally came at Christmastime. On a cold night, the American troops crossed the Delaware River and marched through sleet and rain to Trenton, New Jersey. Washington's soldiers captured a company of Hessians, German soldiers fighting for the British. The Hessians had celebrated quite a bit on Christmas and were still sleeping when Washington's troops arrived. The Continental Army took nearly 1,000 prisoners. The victory gave the patriots' cause a much-needed morale boost.

Spurred on by the victory, Washington's army drove the British from Princeton, New Jersey, in January 1777. Philadelphia was now safe for the congress. In March 1777, Hancock left Dolly and Lydia in Baltimore and headed back to Philadelphia.

Famed painter John Trumbull portrayed the 1777 Battle of Princeton in one of a series of Revolutionary War paintings.

*A 1781 etching
of John Hancock*

The war shifted away from New England and toward the mid-Atlantic states. Because of the shift in fighting, John decided it was safe to send Dolly and the baby to Massachusetts. A few weeks later, however, baby Lydia died of a fever. Her death hit Hancock hard. He was already in poor health and suffered from gout. He missed his wife and mourned Lydia.

The war plodded on. A British force of nearly 8,000 men under General John Burgoyne invaded New York from Canada. The British planned to cut New England off from the rest of the colonies. To counterattack the British move, Hancock spent hours writing letters to various state militias. He asked them to move to protect New England. The American forces lost Fort Ticonderoga, a key position in northern New York. The British also moved into the northern part of the Chesapeake Bay with 15,000 men under General William Howe and planned to take Philadelphia.

The autumn brought the Battle of Brandywine Creek in Pennsylvania. Washington and more than 10,000 troops retreated toward Philadelphia as General Howe's troops attacked. Congress again left Philadelphia. This time, they relocated to nearby Lancaster and then to York, Pennsylvania.

By October 1777, John Hancock had had enough. His poor health plagued him. Repeated attacks of gout caused serious discomfort and made standing or walking painful. Hancock wrote to General Washington and explained his thoughts:

> *It is now above two years since I have had the honour of presiding in Congress, and I should esteem myself happy to have it in my Power to render further Service to my Country in that department. But the decline of health occasioned by so long and unremitting application to the duties of my office, both in Congress and out of Congress, ... has at length, taught me to think of retiring for two or three months.*

On October 29, the 40-year-old John Hancock stood before the Continental Congress to speak. Here is an excerpt from his speech:

> *Gentlemen: Friday last completed two years and five months since you did me the honor of electing me to fill this chair ...*

*My health being much impaired, I find
some relaxation absolutely necessary, after
such constant application, I must therefore
request your indulgence for leave of
absence for two months.*

*But I cannot take my departure, Gentle-
men, without expressing my thanks for the
civility and politeness I have experienced
from you. It is impossible to mention this,
without a heart felt pleasure.*

John Hancock returned to Boston, Beacon Hill,
and Dolly. His requested two-month leave stretched
on. The following year, another child, John George
Washington Hancock was born. The Hancocks
delighted in their son, whom they called Johnny.

As his health slowly improved, John Hancock
took on a new role—assuming command as major
general of the Massachusetts militia. Though he still
had no experience as a military officer, Hancock led
6,000 men toward Rhode Island.

Hancock intended for his troops to help rid
Rhode Island of the British, who had taken over
Newport. Hancock expected to combine his efforts
with the Continental Army and the French naval fleet
anchored off the coast to oust the British. The battle
would, Hancock felt certain, be quickly won.

Speed was essential. Most of Hancock's men were
farmers and had signed up for a short two weeks'
service. Considering the trip to and from Rhode Island,

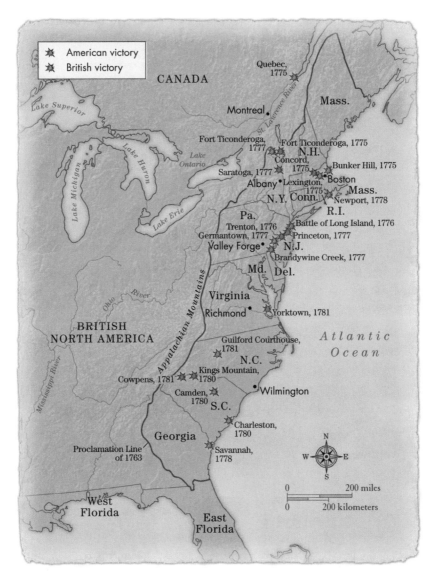

American victory
British victory

CANADA

Quebec, 1775

Mass.

Lake Superior

Montreal

St. Lawrence River

Fort Ticonderoga, 1777

Fort Ticonderoga, 1775

N.H.

Lake Ontario

Concord, 1775

Saratoga, 1777

Bunker Hill, 1775

Albany•Lexington, Boston
1775

Mass.

N.Y. Conn. Newport, 1778

R.I.

Lake Michigan

Lake Huron

Lake Erie

Pa.

Trenton, 1776

Germantown, 1777

Valley Forge•

Battle of Long Island, 1776

Princeton, 1777

N.J.

Brandywine Creek, 1777

Md. Del.

Ohio River

Virginia

Richmond•

•Yorktown, 1781

BRITISH
NORTH AMERICA

Appalachian Mountains

Guilford Courthouse, 1781

Atlantic
Ocean

N.C.

Kings Mountain, 1780

Cowpens, 1781

Camden, 1780

•Wilmington

S.C.

Mississippi River

Georgia

Charleston, 1780

Proclamation Line
of 1763

Savannah, 1778

N

W   E

S

0   200 miles

West
Florida

0   200 kilometers

East
Florida

the Newport attack could last only a couple of days.
The battle for Newport was a disaster. Terrible weather,
disorganization, and not enough troops played key
roles in the failure. Hancock quickly headed home. ✍

*Major battles of
the Revolution
were fought
throughout
the colonies.*

9 GOVERNOR OF MASSACHUSETTS

❧

Even though the war had not ended and American victory was not certain, the colonies went ahead with their plans for independence from England. The newly formed Commonwealth of Massachusetts developed its own constitution. The document set rules for governing the commonwealth and included the election of a governor. John Adams wrote the document, which then went to all Massachusetts towns for approval.

Hancock ran for governor and on September 4, 1780, received about 11,000 out of 12,281 votes. John Hancock arrived to take his governor's oath in a red velvet jacket with gold trim and buttons. A company of 100 cadets accompanied his ornate yellow carriage. Some Massachusetts citizens felt that Hancock's

John Adams (1735-1826) was known as a gruff, blunt, outspoken man. A lawyer, politician, rebel, patriot, and, later, U.S. president, John Adams helped negotiate the peace treaty that ended the Revolutionary War. Adams died on July 4, 1826, the same day as Thomas Jefferson and the 50th anniversary of American independence.

taking office more closely resembled crowning a king.

Hancock's first speech to a joint session of the Massachusetts legislature took place on October 31, 1780. He asked the members to provide for a larger militia. "Of all the weighty business that lies before you, a point of the first importance and most pressing necessity is the establishment of the Army ... with such seasonable and competent supplies as may render it ... [an effective] defense to the free Constitutions and Independence of the United States."

Hancock mentioned a number of issues he considered important. He wanted all Massachusetts children to have an education, so building schools was important. The war had left many widows and orphans, and these people needed state help. The commonwealth required new roads, public buildings, and schools. These efforts required money.

With no money in the bank, the commonwealth passed laws to collect taxes on property. The new taxes angered the citizens. They were fighting a war against Great Britain over taxes, and now their new government was passing laws to collect them!

Hancock sympathized with the citizens, but the commonwealth needed money.

The American Revolution continued to drag on. By 1781, however, the British forces had reached a point of collapse. The determined American forces nipped at British heels at every turn. As summer ended, the British found themselves caught between a rock and a hard place—or, more accurately, between the Chesapeake Bay and a combined force of nearly 17,000 American and French troops. The Yorktown, Virginia, siege brought an end to the war when British General Charles Cornwallis raised a white flag for a cease-fire on October 17, 1781.

John Trumbull's painting of the British surrender at Yorktown hangs in the Capitol rotunda in Washington.

Treaty discussions continued for nearly two years. Finally, Great Britain and the United States signed the Treaty of Paris on September 3, 1783. Britain recognized the United States of America as an independent country. For those who had taken part in the momentous events of the past eight years, the victory was truly sweet. Hancock, Adams, Jefferson, and the other signers of the Declaration of Independence witnessed the beginnings of a great nation.

The Treaty of Paris bears the signatures of Benjamin Franklin and John Adams, among others.

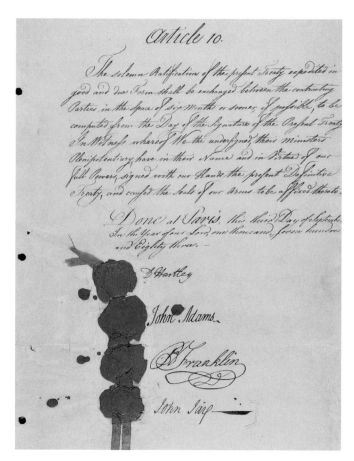

Yet all was not well with Hancock. For more than a year, he had been suffering ill health. His gout grew worse, his joints swelled, and he endured terrible pain. At times, he could not even hold a pen in his hand. By 1784, Hancock could not campaign for reelection as governor, yet he won easily. Too crippled to walk or stand on his own, Hancock governed the state from a wheelchair. In January 1785, Hancock resigned as governor. The task of running the state wore him down too much. Although he was reelected to the Continental Congress and was named its president, he could not attend the sessions.

For the next few years, Hancock remained at home. His health did not allow him to do much else. His legs became so swollen that he often could not dress and go out in public. He could barely walk and needed help climbing stairs and moving about the family home. He spent many days reading to his son and enjoying a close family life.

While Hancock remained at home, Massachusetts' citizens grew weary of Governor James Bowdoin's leadership. They blamed him for the high taxes that pushed farmers deep into debt. In 1786, farmers asked the commonwealth government to issue paper money, reduce their tax debts, and protect them from losing their farms over those debts.

At one protest, the mob of unhappy farmers grew rowdy. Governor Bowdoin sent 600 militia to stop the protest. Farmer Daniel Shays led 1,200 rebels in an event that is called Shays' Rebellion. Throughout Massachusetts, farmers banded together and rioted. The governor called out more troops.

The militia faced the farmers at Petersham, Massachusetts. Shots were fired. Four of Shays' followers lay dead. The militia captured 150 rebels as Shays fled to New Hampshire. Shays' Rebellion made

A rebel and a government supporter fought during Shays' Rebellion.

the legislature think twice about passing new taxes.

After the dangers of Boston's rebellion and the American Revolution, Hancock never expected disaster to strike his quiet Beacon Hill home life. In January 1787, his 8-year-old son Johnny went ice-skating on a nearby pond. Johnny fell and struck his head on a rock. Friends carried the unconscious boy home, where he later died. John and Dolly ached from their loss.

Public service offered an opportunity for John Hancock to get his mind off of his son's death. He was once again elected governor and took office in April. Shays' Rebellion was still fresh in his mind. His sympathy lay with the farmers, who had worked so hard and risked so much to protest unfair taxes. Perhaps Hancock recognized himself in the faces of the rebels. He, too, had worked hard and risked much for his country's freedom.

In June, Hancock, through the courts, granted full pardons for all Shays' rebels. He also pushed through new laws that protected a debtor's personal property. While this made Hancock more popular with common citizens, it enraged businessmen. If a debtor could not be jailed and his property seized, what would force payment of debts, they wondered.

Hancock's next challenge became the battle over the Constitution of the United States. In September 1787, the Constitutional Convention agreed to a document that would establish the laws of the nation. The Constitution began with this preamble:

> *We the people of the United States, in order to form a more perfect union, establish justice, insure domestic tranquility, provide for the common defense, promote the general welfare, and secure the blessings of liberty to ourselves and our posterity, do ordain and establish this Constitution for the United States of America.*

The document was sent to each state for ratification. The first states to approve the new constitution were Delaware, Pennsylvania, New Jersey, Georgia, and Connecticut.

In Massachusetts, representatives met at a convention to discuss the document. Two sides arose to put forth their views. On one side were the Federalists. They favored a strong national government, with less power held by the states. The anti-Federalists took the opposite view—they wanted states to be stronger and the federal government to be weaker. An early voting poll showed that the anti-Federalists would win, 192 votes to 144. If that happened, Massachusetts would not approve the U.S. Constitution.

However, as president of the Massachusetts Constitutional Convention, John Hancock did not allow the matter to come to a vote so quickly. He and other politicians suggested that nine amendments to the Constitution be proposed. These amendments would guarantee certain personal rights. Eventually, these nine amendments, plus one more, became the Bill of Rights. One amendment guaranteed freedom of religion, speech, and the press. Another allowed for forming a militia for protection. Others protected people's homes from unreasonable searches and guaranteed speedy trials by jury.

John Hancock's suggestion of amendments eased the way for approval of the Constitution in Massachusetts.

Even the anti-Federalists could agree that, with the amendments added, the new document served both the government and the people. When Massachusetts voted at last, the Constitution was ratified by 187 votes to 168. Again, Hancock's ability to work with people served the state and nation well.

John Hancock is buried at the Old Granary Burying Ground in Boston.

With the Constitution question resolved, it was time to elect a president of the United States. George Washington was an obvious choice. He was well known and had proved his ability to lead. He had the respect of people in every state. Some suggested that Hancock be elected vice president. However, his health had declined so much that further service to the country was impossible.

For the remainder of his life, Hancock governed Massachusetts from his house on Beacon Hill and rarely left home. He died October 8, 1793, while serving his ninth term as governor. He was 56 years old.

During his life, Hancock knew great wealth, pain, and loss. In his personal life, he enjoyed a successful marriage, but suffered the loss of both his children. Publicly, Hancock led his state into a rebellion and risked his wealth and safety for the cause of freedom. Hancock urged his country to independence and became one of its founding fathers. He helped set up a democratic form of government, which stands strong to this day. ✎

HANCOCK'S LIFE

1737

January 12, John Hancock is born in Braintree (now Quincy), Massachusetts

1744

Adopted by his Uncle Thomas and Aunt Lydia, making him heir to the Hancock business empire

1754

Graduates from Harvard College

1735   1750

1749

German writer Johann Wolfgang Goethe is born

1738

Englishman John Wesley and his brother Charles found the Methodist church

1756–63

The Seven Years' War is fought; Britain defeats France

WORLD EVENTS

1764

Thomas Hancock dies and John inherits the House of Hancock

1765

Colonists protest the Stamp Act and Hancock joins the protest

1767

Leads a merchant boycott of British goods

1764

James Hargreaves creates the spinning jenny, a mechanical spinning wheel

HANCOCK'S LIFE

1773
Boston Tea Party
protests a tax on tea

1770
Boston Massacre
shocks the citizens of
Massachusetts

1768
Tried as a smuggler
by the British

1770

1769
British explorer
Captain James Cook
reaches New Zealand

1772
Poland is partitioned
for the first time,
between Russia,
Prussia, and Austria

WORLD EVENTS

1775

Becomes president of
the Second Continental
Congress and marries
Dorothy Quincy

1774

Speaks at the Boston
Massacre memorial

1776

Signs the Declaration
of Independence;
daughter Lydia
Hancock is born

1775

1774

King Louis XV of
France dies and his
grandson, Louis XVI
is crowned

1776

Scottish economist
Adam Smith publishes
The Wealth of Nations,
heralding the beginning
of modern economics

Life and Times

HANCOCK'S LIFE

1780-1785
Serves as
Massachusetts governor

1777
Lydia Hancock dies

1778
John George
Washington Hancock
is born

1780

1779
Jan Ingenhousz of the
Netherlands discovers
that plants release
oxygen when exposed
to sunlight

1783
The first manned
hot air balloon flight
is made in Paris,
France, by the
Montgolfier
brothers

WORLD EVENTS

1788

Proposes nine amendments, which become the beginning of the Bill of Rights and help get the U.S. Constitution passed in Massachusetts

1793

October 8, dies in Boston, Massachusetts

1787

Son Johnny dies; Massachusetts again elects Hancock as governor

1790

1788

The *Times* newspaper in London is founded

1791

Austrian composer Wolfgang Amadeus Mozart dies

1786

The British government announces its plans to make Australia a penal colony

DATE OF BIRTH: January 12, 1737

BIRTHPLACE: Braintree (now Quincy), Massachusetts

FATHER: Reverend John Hancock (1702-1744)

MOTHER: Mary Hawke Hancock (1711- 1783)

ADOPTIVE PARENTS: Uncle Thomas and Aunt Lydia Hancock

EDUCATION: Harvard College

SPOUSE: Dorothy (Dolly) Quincy Hancock (1744-1818)

DATE OF MARRIAGE: August 28, 1775

CHILDREN: Lydia Henchman Hancock (1776-1777)
John George Washington Hancock (1778-1787)

DATE OF DEATH: October 8, 1793

PLACE OF BURIAL: Boston, Massachusetts

In the Library

Fradin, Dennis Brindell. *The Signers: The Fifty-six Stories Behind the Declaration of Independence.* New York: Walker & Company, 2002.

Gaines, Ann Graham. *John Hancock: President of the Continental Congress.* Broomall, Pa: Chelsea House, 2000.

Grote, JoAnn A. *The American Revolution.* Broomhall, Pa.: Chelsea House, 1999.

Koslow, Philip. *John Hancock: A Signature Life.* New York: Franklin Watts, 1998.

Ransom, Candice F. *John Hancock.* Minneapolis: Lerner, 2005.

On the Web

For more information on *John Hancock*, use FactHound to track down Web sites related to this book.

1. Go to *www.facthound.com*
2. Type in a search word related to this book or this book ID: 0756508282
3. Click on the *Fetch It* button.

FactHound will find the best Web sites for you.

Historic Sites

The National Archives Building
5700 Pennsylvania Ave., N.W.
Washington, DC 20408
866/272-6272
To view the Declaration of Independence, the Constitution, and the Bill of Rights

Boston Historical Society and Museum
Old State House
206 Washington St.
Boston, MA 02109-1713
617/720-1713
To learn more about the Revolutionary War and its participants

amendment
a change made to a law or legal document

annul
to make legally invalid

apprentice
a person who works for and learns from a skilled tradesperson for a certain amount of time

arsenal
a place where guns and ammunition are made or stored

bayonet
blades attached to the end of rifles and used as weapons in close combat

boycott
a refusal to buy certain goods or services as a form of protest

carnage
bloody slaughter or injury

Constitution
the document stating the basic laws of the United States

customs
taxes on goods brought into a country

gout
a painful health condition that attacks joints

guerrilla
member of an independent military unit carrying out harassment or sabotage

heir
a person who is to receive money or property from someone after that person dies

indigo
a plant that produces a dark blue dye

Glossary

magazine
a room or building where ammunition and explosives are stored

martial law
the act of controlling a country, state, or city by military means

mercenary
hired for service in the army of a foreign country

militia
a loosely organized military group of people

Minutemen
colonists who were ready to grab their guns at a moment's notice

Parliament
the part of the British government that makes laws

pound sterling
the basic monetary unit of Great Britain

ratification
official approval of a law or document

representation
a person or group standing up for a cause or for other people

rod
a unit for measuring that equals 5 ½ yards (5 meters)

siege
the surrounding of an enemy position for a long time to cut off supplies and force a surrender

textile
fabric that is made by weaving or knitting

treason
an attempt to betray one's own country

Chapter 1
Page 9, line 10: Declaration of Independence.

Page 13, line 4: George Brown Tindall, with David E. Shi. *America: A Narrative History*, 3rd ed. New York and London: W.W. Norton and Co., 1992, p. 212.

Chapter 3
Page 27, line 5: Thomas Hancock. A Letter to J. Barnard, January 1, 1763. Massachusetts Historical Society.

Page 30, line 2: Molasses Act, May 17, 1773.

Chapter 5
Page 47, line 4: "An Account of the Late Military Massacre at Boston, March 1770." http://lcweb2.loc.gov/learn/features/timeline/amrev/brittwo/account.html.

Page 48, sidebar: Thomas Paine. *Liberty Tree*. http://www.constitutional.net/152.html.

Page 51, line 20: John Hancock. A Letter to J. Barnard, December 21, 1773. Massachusetts Historical Society.

Chapter 6
Page 57, line 11: Harlow Giles Unger. *John Hancock: Merchant King and American Patriot*. New York: John Wiley & Sons, 2000, p. 186.

Page 59, line 14: Sylvanus Wood. "Battle at Lexington Green, 1775," http://www.eyewitnesstohistory.com/lexington.htm.

Page 61, line 7: "Eyewitness Accounts: Major John Pitcairn. *Revolutionary Viewpoints.* www.wviz.org/edsvcs/Revolutionary_Viewpoints/pitcairn.html.

Page 62, line 2: "Biography: Dorothy Quincy Hancock." www.colonialhall.com/hancock/hancockDorothy.php.

Chapter 7
Page 67, line 8: Henry Collins Walsh. "Three Letters from Hancock to "Dorothy Q." cdl.library.cornell.edu/cgi-bin/moa/.

Page 70, line 19: Ibid.

Page 71, line 22: Herbert S. Allen. *John Hancock, Patriot in Purple*. New York: Beechurst Publishing, 1953, p. 210.

Chapter 8
Page 76, line 15: Edmund C. Burnett, ed. Letters of Members of the Continental Congress. Washington, D.C.: The Carnegie Institution in Washington, 1921–1936, vol. 2., p. 286.

Page 81, line 12: John Hancock. A Letter to George Washington, October 17, 1777. George Washington Papers at the Library of Congress, Series 4, p. 924.

Page 81, line 26: Paul D. Brandes. *John Hancock's Life and Speeches*. Lanham, Md.: The Scarecrow Press, Inc., 1996, pp. 234-235.

Chapter 9
Page 86, line 7: Ibid., p 240.

Page 92, line 3: U.S. Constitution, preamble.

Allen, Herbert S. *John Hancock, Patriot in Purple.* New York: Beechurst Publishing, 1953.

Autobiography of John Adams. Adams Family Papers: An Electronic Archive. http://www.masshist.org/digitaladams/aea/autobio/.

Brandes, Paul D. *John Hancock's Life and Speeches.* Lanham, Md.: The Scarecrow Press, Inc., 1996.

Burnett, Edmund C., ed. *Letters of Members of the Continental Congress.* Washington, D.C.: The Carnegie Institution in Washington, 1921–1936, vol. 2.

"Eyewitness Accounts: Major John Pitcairn." *Revolutionary Viewpoints.* www.wviz.org/edsvcs/Revolutionary_Viewpoints/pitcairn.html.

Fowler, William M. *The Baron of Beacon Hill.* Boston: Houghton Mifflin Co., 1976.

Hancock, John. A Letter to J. Barnard, December 21, 1773. Massachusetts Historical Society.

Hancock, John. A Letter to George Washington, October 17, 1777. George Washington Papers at the Library of Congress, Series 4, p. 924.

Hancock, Thomas. A Letter to J. Barnard, January 1, 1763. Massachusetts Historical Society.

Koslow, Philip. *John Hancock: A Signature Life.* Danbury, Conn.: Franklin Watts, 1998.

Morris, Richard B., and Jeggrey B. Morris, eds. *Encyclopedia of American History.* New York: Harper Collins, 1996.

Schlesinger, Arthur M., Jr., ed. *The Almanac of American History.* New York: Barnes & Noble Books, 1993.

Tindall, George Brown, and David E. Shi. *America: A Narrative History*, 3rd ed. New York and London: W.W. Norton and Co., 1992.

Unger, Harlow Giles. *John Hancock: Merchant King and American Patriot.* New York: John Wiley & Sons, 2000.

U.S. National Archives and Records Administration.

U.S. Congressional Documents and Debates, 1774-1875. Journals of the Continental Congress.

Walsh, Henry Collins. "Three Letters from Hancock to 'Dorothy Q.'" cdl.library.cornell.edu/cgi-bin/moa/.

Barbara A. Somervill has been writing for more than 30 years. She has written newspaper and magazine articles, video scripts, and books for children. She enjoys writing about science and investigating people's lives for biographies. She is an avid reader and traveler. Ms. Somervill lives with her husband in South Carolina.

Image Credits

U.S. Capitol Historical Society/detail of *The Declaration of Independence* by John Trumbull, cover (top), 4–5, 8, 99 (right); MHS175759 *John Hancock* (1737-93) c. 1770-72 (oil on canvas) by John Singleton Copley (1738-1815), Massachusetts Historical Society, Boston, MA, USA/The Bridgeman Art Library, cover (bottom), 2, 64; Lombard Antiquarian Maps & Prints, 11, 22, 96 (all); Todd A. Gipstein/Corbis, 12; Giraudon/Art Resource, N.Y., 14; The Granger Collection, New York, 19, 84; Paul V. Galvin Library Digital History Collection, 20; National Portrait Gallery, Smithsonian Institution/Art Resource, N.Y., 21; Victoria & Albert Museum, London/Art Resource, N.Y., 24; Mary Evans Picture Library, 27; Burstein Collection/Corbis, 28; Réunion des Musées Nationaux/Art Resource, N.Y., 30; Archivo Iconografico, S.A./Corbis, 32; North Wind Picture Archives, 35, 42, 47, 58, 97 (top); MPI/Getty Images, 36, 49, 56; Library of Congress, 39, 44, 55, 73, 74, 80, 98 (top left), 99 (left), 100 (top), 101 (all); Historical Picture Archive/Corbis, 40; Time Life Pictures/Mansell/Getty Images, 50, 98 (top right); Yale Center for British Art, Paul Mellone Collection/The Bridgeman Art Library, 52; Courtesy of the Director, National Army Museum, London, 60; Photo from the collection of the Lexington, Massachusetts Historical Society, 61; Bettmann/Corbis, 63, 70, 90, 93; National Park Service, Harpers Ferry Center Commissioned Art Collection, artist Don Troiani, 67; Francis G. Mayer/Corbis, 69, 79; The Pierpont Morgan Library/Art Resource, N.Y., 77; U.S. Capitol Historical Society/*Surrender of Lord Cornwallis* by John Trumbull, 87; Corbis, 88; Ted Spiegel/Corbis, 94; Hulton/Archive by Getty Images, 97 (bottom); Wildside Press, 98 (bottom); Index Stock Imagery, 100 (bottom).

306
163